SPRING

UNIVERSITY OF
ILLINOIS PRESS

Urbana and Chicago

spring

poems by ONI BUCHANAN

© 2008 by Oni Buchanan
All rights reserved
Manufactured in the United States
of America
1 2 3 4 5 C P 5 4 3 2 1
∞ This book is printed on
acid-free paper.

Library of Congress
Cataloging-in-Publication Data
Buchanan, Oni
Spring : poems / by Oni Buchanan.
p.   cm. — (The national poetry series)
ISBN 978-0-252-03364-3
(cl. : acid-free paper)
ISBN 978-0-252-07564-3
(pbk. : acid-free paper)
1. Spring—Poetry.
I. Title.
PS3602.U25S67   2008
811'.6—dc22   2008009045

The National Poetry Series

The National Poetry Series was established in 1978 to ensure the publication of five poetry books annually through participating publishers. Publication is funded by Stephen Graham, the International Institute of Modern Letters, the Joyce and Seward Johnson Foundation, the Juliet Lea Hillman Simonds Foundation, the Tiny Tiger Foundation, and Charles B. Wright III. This project is also sponsored by the National Endowment for the Arts, which believes that a great nation deserves great art.

2007 Competition Winners

Joe Bonomo of DeKalb, Illinois, *Installations*
Chosen by Naomi Shihab Nye, published by Penguin Books

Oni Buchanan of Brighton, Massachusetts, *Spring*
Chosen by Mark Doty, published by University of Illinois Press

Sabra Loomis of New York, New York, *House Held Together by Winds*
Chosen by James Tate, published by HarperCollins Publishers

Donna Stonecipher of Seattle, Washington, *The Cosmopolitan*
Chosen by John Yau, published by Coffee House Press

Rodrigo Toscano of Brooklyn, New York, *Collapsible Poetics Theater*
Chosen by Marjorie Welish, published by Fence Books

Acknowledgments

Enormous thanks to Mark Doty, the National Poetry Series, and everyone at the University of Illinois Press for making this book possible, with unfathomable gratitude to the following private sponsors of this book, whose extraordinary contributions made possible the inclusion of the Flash-animation CD of the Mandrake Vehicles: Nancy and Lloyd M. Aiello, M.D., Colleen Hovey and Christopher Bator, Harry and Nicholas Bator, Dr. and Mrs. Charles Evans, Christine Grant, Porter Hall, David Hricik, Sirkku Konttinen and Harri Kytömaa, T. F. Richardson, David Ritchie, Ted Robinson, and Miranda Pratt and D. Christopher Wells. For their indispensable assistance in the production of the Mandrake Vehicles, further gratitude to Jon Sakata, Phillip Pond, and Flash-animator extraordinaire Betsy Stone Mazzoleni.

Grateful thanks to the editors of the following publications in which poems from this book first appeared: *Columbia: A Journal of Literature & Art, Columbia Poetry Review, Conduit, Copper Nickel, Dragonfire, Drunken Boat, Forklift, Ohio, Guernica, Gulf Coast, H_NGM_N Poetry Journal, Joyful Noise: An Anthology of American Spiritual Poetry, jubilat, La Petite Zine, LIT Magazine, past simple, Puella Mea, Seneca Review,* and *three candles journal.* Special thanks to William Waltz and *Conduit* for first publishing the full Flash-animation of the Mandrake Vehicles, and to Jake Adam York and *Copper Nickel* for creating a chapbook of "Or Portals to Another World." Thanks to the Poetry Society of America and the Bread Loaf Writers' Conference for acknowledgment and inspiration.

Thank you to the many friends, colleagues, and teachers past and present who have contributed their steadfast enthusiasm and support for my projects during the writing of this manuscript. In addition to those people already mentioned above, and the many, many others whose kindnesses have contributed to my life and to this book, I would like to thank in particular Thomas Bross, Fred Chappell, Michael Collier, Jay DeWire, Stephen Drury, Daniel Epstein, Richard Greene, Carrie Iverson, Major Jackson, Myna Jayne Joseph, Martin Lammon, Sabrina Orah Mark,

Lisa Mezzacappa, Sara Mueske, Luba Poliak, Elaine Rombola, Aleyson Scopel, Joshua Wolf Shenk, Russell Sherman, Donna Stonecipher, Mimi Tung, Brian Waniewski, Patricia Zander and, not least, Squeakers Tyrell. Thank you to my family for their love and generosity, especially Robin Welte, Art Murray, Kelly and Colette Buchanan, and Pete and Cindy Woodward. Beyond the ability of words to capture gratitude, thank you to Jon Woodward.

Contents

for my teachers

The Smallest Plant

And is there a greater hero than the least plant that grows?
—John Cage, from "Experimental Music"

And what strength precedes the sun
rising, makes the desire to rise
master the beaten down?
For the bleak dosage daily is
administered: the deputy office of a
so-called God inflicts
its shallow law— Oh, hear what
the smallest plant uttered rising to meet
a single thin beam penetrating:
Spring?

The Floor-Creatures Begin

The skin was stretched tauter, fastened
through the metal hoop—membrane of sky over the earth's
frame—and the sun struck its last hour
with a mallet wrapped in violet yarn,
tones that rose to the surface, the red swirls
deepening to violet (the disturbed blood darkening)
and outward in shade to the boundaries
(a deep tumultuous sleep)
until the skein grew dark to its edges
(a consuming sleep of coughs).

      (And the sound, some dry kindling burning,
      the crisp, the tiny sputtering,
      rupture of the throat into sediment and sod.
      It could be the desiccated remnants of stems
      in the harvested field. It could be
      a lean-to of sticks, and then the deaf,
      burning that which they call unsacred.
      The deaf, dividing and dividing again
      that smallest vial of God's voice—)

Between the ground, between the sky,
the animals call out. A velveteen ear, the black air
quivering: the pine needles gathered in a spur.
And how what was spoken, too, expanded to the running edges—
the tundra, the vast veldt, the funnel of black wings
landing on the rock en masse, a smoothing,
a soothing of black, the indivisible plumage
and the mass of black flies hovering over an arctic wave.

Over the ocean a white bird drops out of the sky
then flies up again, out, wet with a writhing
piece from the volume, and the volume
seals over, and the hole fills itself
with spill from around—

      (What, like an army of needles, if all the white birds fell at once
      from their formation, a decided drop,
        if all the white birds banked steep to the sun-eye to dive
      like venom-tipped stingers, sore for the job.
      Sore as the disheveled petals of lilies,
      as the rubbed lens of the netherworld tread on,
      and then the white wings skewered from the water, strung
      like sails for a body.
      The floor-creatures begin then
      to desire. A dagger to the hilt of water—)

The teeming liquid curls in—   But inside the umbrage
of the curve, in the lining of its velvet furl: a thought
of petal—is it you, viscous address
of the center of flowers? Dusted on the fine,
the gathering legs? Dusted on the tongue, a seeding
to blossom? (Is it you,
underwhisper of song? Open; tell me again—)

Song Cycle

Song of the voice, mellifluous song, delight
of the breath. The noise of the unbuttoning
will commence from underneath, the organs

casting off their fumes of exhaust, a decay we can shape
to the language we exchange, dying— The sound
differs, as always, as always—vaporous, and

the water, spilling from the curved
borders of the body. *There was a day,*
perhaps not even a full day, as the moon

waned, as the interchangeable bodies collide on a field
and leave behind them
the interchangeable bodies. Dull thuds

from within the glass jar (one must surround
the ear with glass, trembling like a
marsh marigold in its globe). Blood to be gathered

in thimbles. So many lit windows,
and the dark flow between, a current with the bodies
enfolded, those that fell without so much

as a whisper to the night, or to the water
which seduced with its susurrous slippage—
(The swannery, where swallowtails swaggered on swards—)

Like dew-embers, the suspirations. The spruce
bedazzling with its scents swirling, an essence distilled.
And the plangent cry

of the boughs! And the tundra swans trumpeting!
The yearlings in the migratory line. Oh stillness, your safe,
your chiseled hand—let the birds land upon it

and leave again, an acrobat's smile—

Amaryllis

As for structure, the stones formed a grid,
a matrix of space—stones: room
for water, room for air—stones: the roots grow
through you and tether you to their heart.
For yet the red banners there lie flag-folded and bound.
For the full-blown amaryllis a wayward bloom
whose heavy awe leeches light from the white
air to host its depraved trumpets' blare.
Deafening, they intone angels' anthems, red-robed,
and wave censers to smother a breath less
than fire, a breath that lets a pure
molecule enter, no conflagration of bodies, no
worshippers' wounds proud-flown and waved.
Here you lie, myopic bulb of a saturating
reign, not yet flashes and top-heavy glare,
still quiet, uncharted and set like a stone
among stones. Like the cold pure world
layered into the land in limestone and slate, shale
and granite, basalt, diorite, sandstone, flint—

The Sleepers

And in the dimness of the corridor, a waking person steps
soundlessly through the rows of unseen sleepers, each
in his individual box behind a wall.

Another treads elsewhere, a parallel corridor, a carpet
of deep maroon absorbing the weight of the step,
the sound of the step, as if no one—

The gray wears a gray scarf, knitted, about its throat,
or seeps from itself, evaporating into gray, a mist, heapings of insulation,
    the itch
of material, gray swathe, stiff canvas of filament—and above,
outside the hallways (rectangular prisms of gray) (two telescopes of gray
    capped on either end):
the dull stars stuck over the earth like buttons in a dust upholstery.

And sing soft to one another, and the bodies follow from offstage,
from behind the heavy plush, where the ropes are held and the hands
    dressed in black
flit between the long, thin planes of scenery—

> *On the path we saw a tanager like an orange handkerchief pulled
>   through the leaves.*
> There is always that distant tremolo in the air that rises from
>   the green,
> from the graves in the dell,
> and the kingfisher diving over the membrane of pond.
>
> And above all the tangle (the matted earth, the root hairs and
>   vascular
> bundles, the barky breachings of gnarl, the bullfrogs and the
>   gnat-clouds,

the squirrels growing fatter, and then the panoplies of
    leaves-on-leaves
like a game of stacking hands, or canopies

where the branches arch in ribs), *above*:
the spots of chimney sparrows flitting like eye motes over
    the white of the sky.
The rattle of the sparrows like a handful of dice
or dried beans thrown into a toy drum

(the sound of the rattle like a hemisphere of straight pins
radiating from their cushion, the pin heads balancing each
its million spots of light, allotted, while beneath
and down to the sharpened tip, the long metal shafts
vibrate invisibly: *sleep*.

Sleep. Sleep. Your separate sleeps—)

Vespers

Each escaped by district, the lonely
welding of bones—Forgive
us: we punish ourselves, each
our Mondrian chambers arranged—
the rank, the fetid breath
impenetrable, wet, kept.
Each our hypnotic rite
to outdo yellowing days, the haze
that clouds the edge of hours.
For the sundowns seep into the dawns lest we
remark them, lest each his
tarnished isolated blade whet
to knick a rift into the too-smooth
surface, ration minutes into wells
to shape a message—an artifact—
answer—a clue?

And on the Seventh Day*

after Harry Partch

And on the seventh day, petals fell in Petaluma, and the sky that day
like a snow dome shaken, and the weird instruments built with gourds
and the leather from worn saddles, built with guillotine blades, nuclear
cloud chambers, fuel tanks, and the carved prows of canoes
hollowed from logs—and the instruments spaced beneath the sky
as the petals rained, scraps of velvet in reds and deep magenta and
    whites
like the wings of tiny birds clipped to dwindle
from the bodies of birds hung above the clouds.

And between the patches of color softly descending in velvet address,
a scarlet tanager wheeling like a mad arrow shot from a bow carved
    of antlers,
a tanager like an unsheathed heart flung into the fever of falling color.

And far downward in the valley, the soldiers
lugging such indescribable velvet, a portage of fragrance to infuse in
    the water, miles
from the trudging, on the far side of mountains.

I asked the bird who sung from beneath his brilliant plumage,
does he sing to hear his song in answer, or how
is the *alone* directed (the alone in arrows, across to pierce,
the alone in petals, a soft vaporous downward)—does the song
arise from abandon, and in the abandon, is there
a hope, a secret—such, would that the light

be shared? Or would the new body arrived
quench the first to silence? And the light: of what
liquid light, an amber tasting of honeysuckle, of what metal bent
from the gun shafts down, from the belts of ammunition and
    the petals

falling into upturned bottles? Or if the silence, is it
a radiant—a center in rays—and does the white of it shine,
and with another, the arising, does the shining
silence buoy the new soul?

And on the Seventh Day Petals Fell in Petaluma is the title of a
musical composition by Harry Partch, composed in 1963–64,
and revised in 1966, for instruments of his own invention.

(A) Version

Of all our selves, what if we could choose among
or had to suffer some to surface full-blown
to the present, revived from the burial of
years, as if a fresco's under-drawing rose rust-red
through paint, and visible, this blueprint of a current
scene, a being— Or like nesting dolls, unscrew our torsos
to exhume a younger self, a hatching treacherous by chance,
for perhaps some ancient Vesuvius unearthed to scald,
or some unrecognizable, larval stage appear, some
wide-eyed thing soaking in its equivalent in glass, mistaking
one split self for another, oh possible comrade of the years,
witness to unspoken anecdotes and anguish.
Must we endure confessions from such molding mouths,
parade of variations, garish apparitions—or can I
know you again, lynx-eyed oracle; will you speak
to me, strange beast, beginning, beaten thing
in the language, in the constellation of languages I've forgotten?

A Palimpsest of the Tasks

I look up into a volume of air—it could be
a rectangular prism of air, or require
more, like definition under a behaving surface of curve—
Up through the height of air into space

[space: begins at the boundary
where the black and blacker molecules
outnumber the clear—or where? and on the cusp of it,
how wide is the cusp? Enough to stand on?]—

And within the volume of air,
rising from the visible up, one bird population
and another and a third, stacked
at different altitudes from the earth, fly over

one another, or beneath, each imperceptible
to the other, serene in lines, serene
at the hinge, each in its own
broad amphitheater, looking ahead to the great

tract of air in its continual arrival
like a broad cloth feeding through, a canvas becoming
so near that the brushstrokes of paint appear
as themselves, material in rilles

and ridges, fissures, gulfs, striations—in their own, alien
substantiality, weird in dried clots or sputtering out—
And the panel of the same earth below, a new
terrain from every stratum, kaleidoscope of patches.

And so to lower through
the scrawled layers: a palimpsest of the tasks
of living creatures: the free, luxuriant foliage,
the canopy of green in crazed array, and beneath,

all the small animals going about their gatherings and errands.
The animals sunning themselves on leaves
or clinging to the undersides of mothers.
And beneath, the multiplicity of crawling things, each in its own

crevice, below layers of bark, gnawing, and the xylem
delivering its nutrients to the vascular
outgrowths, and below, through the silicate mantle,
the core wrapped in molten plasma, and inside the core—

what is it, scrawled on the inside of iron?

Still-Life with Interior

When steep in pitch I dolorous cry out
and wake from the can't-be of some fever-
induced dream, some warped confluence of seared
 images, lost entities—the *sound*: sudden
and strange, as if a stolen voice lived to shriek
 in me, white-knuckled and bent to harbor
wildness, tooth and growl. It bristles out
camaraderie, though what's to say its sadness,
 rage aren't mine as lethally. All is
black and blank at bedside. Another human creature
lies in line beside and breathes as I breathe, our
 exhales rising in obelisks that mark our sleep
to those who pass invisibly— Mourners from another
 world. Hush. Let them to our
remnant days submit their tears, coveting
an hour, an instant to re-live. For they feel
 nothing now. I waver in the waking
 dream, a phantom to myself, unlit. And swear
again: if I can weather yet another sleepless
 night, this banishment from all serenity,
 in morning, I'll amalgamate the primal thing
to me, hold it still in fire till molten it form itself to shape
beneath my skin; against.

And of the Words Afterwards

And afterwards, what: a crowd of vacant cells?—the offered words
catapulted from their husks on filaments,
tethers to the far, the desiccated, body, or a hope

unraveling, hope of return—and the sound of the voice
decaying in the atmosphere to an inaudible flat,
the membranes of sound like wineskins, emptied each

of the perceptible tones, and some animal, a badger or fox,
left trotting across its expanse of land, a fording amidst the wisps
of shapes evaporating in the air, and the spilling sounds

thinning more and more faint, meant now
for other, for the smaller
ears, directions to the unfurling blossom, for you,

honeybee of the miles, for you, inchworm toward
the leafbud— And now the ants lining up to trespass,
and now the spinnerets oiled, now the chimney swifts

a rattling in the sky, adrift—though the scent of the cut
still lingers— But if the wisps gathered, if a bouquet
of long slender stems—the voice, is it really gone?

(Or, other, do the emptied vessels sink, filling
with the sky-weight, do they
gather, condense in dermis, settling sheer

onto the grass, the left vellum aloft
on new blades for inscription—?)
The river carries the dropped petals away

from the reflection of branches and out toward the center,
to the sky's reflection—the petals like colored sails
for the liquid wind of that sky—

II

Envelopes of Sky

If I had forgotten,
here they are again,
the invisible (transparent)
envelopes of sky,
clear vesicles and
spheres infused
with scent, intoxi-
cating: the rotting leaves
layering close, closer
to the earth (a moss,
spent, a rust and burn),
the fetid pond with
its excrement of geese,
the coins of rain
through the gutter grates,
the cold clean
hint of the moon,
like water, a wetness
of half-sharp blades,
a weariness,
then grass—cut—
and in pockets, an attar:
the ravished elixir
leaking from night flowers,
as from a gash, a knick
in velvet, and from the thin
injury, the liquor
beading at the seam,
it a mere
constituent in the mix,
the scent of dying—this,

the sky, I'd
wanted pure, I'd meant
the swirling orbs of air
as each a reservoir
in which to disappear,
I'd thought, and there—
to breathe?—

Like a Near Fold

In the courtyard, a matted
chunk of feathers
lies on the walkway,
some membrane
tethering a few
unkempt shafts.

The burgeoning generators
billow their vaporous heave
while the drainage system
mingles old rains,
coins in a pewter jar.

For there were those we did not see nor did we hear
but felt, as soundlessly they passed behind,
close as an exhale and with the tall swaying of grasses

For the skin so delicate, as petals,
that through the white, a glowing rose up,
a blue net surfacing

from where from where

or from how much deeper
than *beneath*, than the fathoms
of an eye, that the needlepoint pierced
from below, that the skin stretched
on its scaffolding of bones
lets the piercing pass, as from
the inmost chamber of the heart

For it comes as carrying an abacus of teeth
beneath the flap of its satchel,
capped in gold, the strung enamel rattling

For it seeps as if nectar sang words,
the wax in melted mounds of color

For the patterned scraps of fabric
stacked on a tack, ripped from source,
its single threads loosening
at the bounds

For from *without*, the warmth
a velour at times, a liquid
shroud for the body—
that like a nearer skin, one
(too tired or cold, too cold)

may turn toward
that it envelop, enfold,
a smooth

entry like a pleat in air, there
all the while, patient
to clasp, like a last
lover, sweet
in its wait, soft,

most of all soft—

Sublimation Attempt

—though in the swathe
of black magnolia we had drifted
up, up, away from the sod, up
the silken whip of scent,
the labyrinth of gardens
receding below, corroded
etching—and climbed
and rose—oh, even past
the honeysuckle drench,
a balm, a drowsy
soporific for the earthly,
but for the waking,
a buoyancy, the medium
for floating up with
flutter-kick, with wings—

And then the inaudible song
begins again, below,
(munch, an underbreath
of grass-eaters)—
Like the finest probe,
it arrives, an invisible
line of metal, asking
where the black frame of sky
tilts askew,
where inchlings of day
leak through: the fume
of too many molecules.
The visible rot,
a harvest of organs—

So dawn interrupts,
for the light returns us
abrupt to dust, leaves us
embers for the ground:
to settle back
to ashen, our core
cooled, shedding inevitable
degrees, for the dirt
bleeds from us
our feverish heat, our
capacity to pass
through matter, call it the
sublime—to evaporate
in wisps, or limb out into
bark, or fester to a hiss, no,
co-conspirator of disappear, I
missed again. I missed.

Solstice

It was hard to hear through the roaring of the wasps.
The dress tighter over the laced corset,
the breath inside smaller at the core.

I found a wing not attached to any bird.
It was lying in the middle of the street,
still soggy with the morning's rain.

An exceptional calculation of berries per starling.
A startling concentration of exhumations per buried.
And marks on the skin

where the electric spine lay underneath.
Calcification. One day, the moon will fly
out of its orbit, a release

like a snapping, an amputation, and the dead rock
gone. The small voices of the lambs
drowned out by the

machinery rigged for their removal.
I began to think about the ocean.
I begged to think, melodic apparitions

rising out of the static chord.
For there is an ocean with huge stones underneath, the shapes
of dinosaurs. Some days, I can't wait

for him to come back for me.
This time I will tell him my new name.
If you are proud of me, I will say,

take me with you. Don't leave me again.

Where Are They Now, Unwilling Friends

What visions do they see in Siberian snow-storms?
What hallucinations in the circle of the moon?

—Anna Akhmatova, from *Requiem, Dedication*

The swans are angry, their beating wingtips studded in ice

> *for rust leaks from the heart, bleeds*
> *outward from the skin,*
> *the putrid ring opening*
> *like a mouth in the sky—*

The last dandelion seeds blow from heaven, a dead field of stalks

> *pock mark where the sky*
> *was immunized*
> *against the earth*

Scales fall from the blind white eye of the sun—what can it see
through the frenzy of its own scales falling?

> *a moth-eaten hole in the wool*
> *blanket we stretch to*
> *cover our shivering*

The innards torn loose and thrown to the wind, skins
not sent to be burned, but resold, sewn for a new
body, animal with black glass eyes

> *I will trade you this quarter*
> *for that quarter*

Or nail clippings of the dead, yellowed and blunt
against our up-turned faces

> *for the scars on her face*
> *told a far different story, the scars*
> *on her scalp, concealed beneath hair*

Who dares scratch the porcelain face, its rashed skin
flaking off in bit, white chips, a downpour of scab

> *her face veiled in a lace*
> *embroidered with black dragonflies*

So cold, so cold, they arrive with white teeth shining
"I remember you from the ocean," I cry out, which makes them laugh
I was only a child then, and the white birds wheeled over the icy sea

> *occluded mother-of-pearl*
> *button, unfastened*
> *thing languishing*
> *in dark pleats*

Shout into the sky and your voice
taken by its static grid, pulled like a coarse
wool from your throat

> *The color in a glass marble*
> *ribbons from the core—*
> *as the iris of an eye rises too*
> *in folds, ruffle of charged blue*
> *that cloaks a pinpoint aperture*

(the color inside unreachable except some long glass needle
draw out, extract the fascination—)

> *within the head, a crank to be*
> *wound, for the regimented music*
> *must play, for the teeth in the cylinder*
> *grate against the metal tines*
> *and a melody, memory, emerges*

What collision spilled the dust of you, unhinged your mahogany urn?
White ash, as if clean; gray ash, as if old

> *An apprentice drew the contour map*
> *with charcoal*

When he stopped asking for me, my name became syllables
of uncharged sound that fell from each other unattracted and cold,
scales of butterfly wings napkined from a spider's lips

The Word

And the moon folds the spoken notes
away. Files into nether.
And if the word immersed in water
is uttered, it fractures

into cells, the seamless bubbles
rising, each a vehicle for the single
syllable, an allotment of breath
severed from the rest—

And to burst would give voice
in bit, the cacophonous pieces
breaching the surface, a tangle,
a flooded exhumation of limbs.

And if the word pronounced in snow,
so should the wet clots adhere
forming the white bodies of birds, eyeless—
And they fly, colliding

into the others' rising, each trying first
to reach the warmth,
each with a shivering wing.
For there was an old outline etched

in the sky, like a coin burned in.
Ancient. And beaming down,
there spread in pools on the ground
the moon-shadows: each fluctuating blot

like a different planetary water
in which to step, submerge—
and each waterhole with its own populations
of the animals arriving, the animals,

thirsty with desire— And to step into, follow
through the other side of depth: all's
drenched, the combs ooze honey, all the sap veins
overbrimmed, clear, and the hemisphere

here a snow dome for the embalmed
world. The lungs breathe sweet,
a nectar for the gods, and fill— The capillaries
glow with gold, a liquid pulse, a spill, for here

the limpid light is drawn (lured)
as venom is drawn: lengthening, as a melting
bead of glass, adored, and the new
steep scent, too: lengthening toward—

Or Portals to Another World

By day the cloud-shadows

fell on wooded hills.

The deciduous terrain claimed

uncharted shadow-lakes in the tops of trees,

the nomadic shapes passed from leaves to leaves

as dictated by a wind, or by the fringe

of sky that drew a bath of dark

(secluded cradle), or by a general

of sun who sent the signals as alarums

for the gathering of armies—

By night, the shadows fell again

but protean black onto black—

A doorway opened up a crack—

—and the pilots bomb

        —the faces (the flesh of faces)

from incredible height above

        sheared from bodies— A face

the city, incinerating all

        chews another face, a limp face

its boulevards and buildings,

        in pleats from its mouth.

landscaping, industrial

        A face hangs like a rag

matrices—and no one runs,

        from a pointed stick driven hard

no animal howls

        into the ground, a stake to measure

at piles of brick,

        property. And over the face of the sun,

not a thing escapes,

        two faces hang, their scalloped

attempts— The pilots land

        edges fluttering in the breeze.

in embers to crawl

        Some faces have so many

exhausted into neat, provided

        holes from the chewing, the

beds. *TWELVE HOURS,*

        puncturing, from dragging

barks a captain. And as they

        themselves by teeth

sleep, a host of unknown

        over the beach of broken

creatures surfaces to build again

        shells (a beach whose ocean

a different city in the first

        long ago receded) that acrobatic

one's place, a general surveys the

        lines of flies angle through,

finished land, plants coordinates

        threading faces together

for threats and whispers

        in their flight paths. The buzzing

missions in a handheld player.

        of the flies disturbs the ones with ears,

And waking into new demand,

        ears heavy and fleshy, tugging down

each pilot plunges direct

        the corners of the eyes, tugging

into adrenaline, and from

        the forehead and the cheeks to fold

his cramped cockpit,

        great channels where the tears

from his helmet humid

        can flow, the irrigation of that desiccated

with his quickened breath,

        earth. On a steppe, faces balance.

flies high enough above

        The cruel faces slide wet

that the target grows surreal

        from birthing sacks, and drenched,

and still, and there he locks

        set off away, designing—   One face

the enemy as numbers

        grinds its teeth in its sleep,

in the crosshairs and feels again

        if you could call its constant trembling,

his heart, deafening inside

        its refusal to open its eyes, "sleep."

his chest, his lungs now breathless

        This is the face that tries to bury

with the deed, his senses sharpened

        itself, waiting for the rain to come

to a super-human sharp, much sharper

        that the parched dust might

than in life, than in some

        forge to mud where it

ordinary life—

        can lay itself down—

Charred, broken stalks,
the blown-out holes,
and the miserables

Only dirt, sky, the deafening
static, and an animal's tracks
gone out of sight

Dawn comes near continuous, for the day much
shorter than the world's day as they

limp with their chosen others
("Others": some
lured sorrowful, some

beneath the lines of noise
(the dusty paw prints
disappear). The crackling

re-enact their dance, their ritual of
appearance. The light in beacon shines, outlines a

puzzler hopeful, maimed
silent for a peer.)
A fashioned tragedy

frays and convulses, ramifies
like a grid of electric wires
low over the ground to

circle on the barren dirt into whose perimeter
the grass blades bend themselves

to share. For each can
tighten tourniquets, gauze
inflicted wounds.

form a hovering
atmospheric wrap, net of
perpetual voltage,

and bow, release their dewdrops and raise to height,
a hoisting by thinnest glimmer-threads left by a diligent spider.

For competence can make
a splint from a former's bone
and set the brokenness—awry—

synaptic code, a buffer for the sky
should a lost thing look
for vantage, should

The violets unfold their stems to reach while
tenor crocuses jut with thicker stalks, the worms appearing

in curve specific to the sick,
the sickened head
to cradle— For competence

a grounded thing
try reaching higher than
itself. The animal was

at the brink of passageways, gnats in pizzicato clouds,
and the beetles metallically arranged to flare the angels down

can balance stone
on stone, a cairn to mark the
spot an old unlucky fell exploded.

deep within, unseen,
unheard, beneath the riddled
air. Not a bleat

(the angels, far above and harnessed to construction cranes,
descend by rope and pulley)

(Inside a stone: a gem!
a secret greed! Inside a stone:
an old volcanic ash—)

or whimper came
from within the buzzing
visionary heart.

And the cold
    seeps into creases—into

creaks—into the thinnest curves of

    metal pieces, crescents

scrupulously cut and laid

in complex polyhedron shapes,

    in flawless ratios
of compartments.

A single sculpted dahlia
    in the midst of mirrors bursts

    into a fractal garden of

reflections. And poised

    on a polished silver table,

a molten mold of lungs swells

    with all the million

branching vessels

Each one, imprisoned in its

    lightless box, seems
black to itself, invisible. Each one

parched and grainy, a hill of motes
    unapplied to any greater

thing, unknowing

    of potential, of the mixing

salve of water, brush, or even color of

    its fluid self, soaring

in the streak, or of its
    properties, an element

for hybrid shades. And is each also

    unaware of other hues

languishing in nearby

motionless and perfect,

each frozen bronchiole forever

drawers? Or do they whisper

to themselves and some days
overhear? Or do they

sing aloud unfinished

content with only its

lines and listen

for a foreign melody
returned? For, haunted,

visions come to each, and

share, its finite vial,

each one isolated dreams

of breath, an inhale ended—

of birds in distant trees, the lost birds

embedded in their leaves like
buttons in a deep

upholstery—

ts heavy
past the dr
plankton c
ations, past
ndering cra
;/all the not
ise up throu
entacles/lik
transport,/
de released

through/se
ongues, sin
a closed fis
/a jellyfish
ing/throug
ts heavy
past the
plankton c
ations; past
ndering cra

/the pulsing
smother th

—for   fatigue   settles   in,   a   must,   a   musk;

the   animals   quiet   now,   soft

vessels   left   behind   for   breeze   to   tousle,

soft   fur   among   the   fluctuating

grasses,   soft   upon   the   hillside   sloping   down—

In   pairs,   the   sexton   beetles

land: *a tiny*   *click,*   *the*   *wing-case*

opens,   *a*   *tiny*   *rustle,*   *a smoothing*   *of*

wings   *folding*   *back*   *beneath*   *the*   *casing—*

The   beetles   whisper   then   the   ritual   lament,

the   elegy   of   trees,   the   liturgy

and   worship.   At   close   of   prayer,   they   dig

a   hole   and   hoist   by   increment

the   chosen   body   to   its

brink.   *How*   *gently*   *they*   *tip*

the   *body*   *in,*   the   smallest   tug

by   ear,   a   prod   of   finest   joint,

and   the   abandoned   nudged   into   the   earth,   a

home.   The   couple   lays   its   eggs   beside,

for   when   the   warm   soul   passes,

the   buried   song   (behind   the   eyes,   beneath

the   tongue)   begins   to   sing,   preparing

newborns   for   the   feast   of   waking,   a   hymn

of   birth   and   paean   for   the   dead,

for   at   the   decomposing   heart,   a   feast   is

found   for   hatching   mouths,   for

at   the   heart,   a   feast—

The Lonely Animal

I visited the animal
I visited it in its hole
I visited it till the dawn
when it sunk its razor teeth
into the dawn's throat, tore,
and the sky began its spill of blood

I visited the animal
I ran down the hillside of wet grass
and found it where it lived
It wasn't sleeping (for it never slept)
It stayed awake all night soundless and still
I visited the animal without a sound

I visited the animal by day
I brought it twigs and ferns
It lashed the branches with a lanyard
woven in and out; it perched upon its bramble throne
It folded closed its sanitary paws, its paws
scrubbed clean down in the cold waters of the stream

I scrubbed with the animal, scrubbed at the stream
scrubbed away the bits of dirt
scrubbed my matted fur, scrubbed
the goblet gilt in gold, the shard of pottery
wedged into the earth; for everything must
be cleaned and readied for the ritual of tears

I drank with the animal, from the gilded goblet
from the cold and flowing stream where
a single goldfish swam: a bright and sudden flash
as quickly gone. The lonely goldfish cries

and its own tears stick to it like sparkling pins
that make it shimmer, like it wears a shawl of diamonds

I cried with the animal
in midday over the water while below
the lily pads gently swooned and shuddered
I cried swooning with the animal
as the evening fell like autumn leaves
as the moss grew damper, deeper and more still

Quiet I watched the animal cry into its goblet
I watched it catch each sliding tear
as carefully as liquid gold
and together they pooled and made a surface
where I was not reflected, where the animal
could watch itself crying, crying, crying—

Dear Lonely Animal,

Please share my Korean food with me.
All the complementary appetizers
in their little white bowls are so delightful.

I arrange them this way and that: a line,
a circle, a zigzag, a pyramid—! I switch their
ordering principles and accessibility

for more amusement. You would love it
here with all this hilarity. And anyway, I'm afraid
to go home by myself even though it's

the middle of the day. Because my house is down
an alley which makes everyone look
suspicious, especially strangers like the roofers

who have been hanging out (when they're not
on the roof) by the enormous Dumpster
they brought with them. How will I fool them

when they watch to see which
of the neighborhood doors I will enter?
How when they grip their nail-guns and

ripping implements, when the frayed
wires spray from beneath the lid of their
mechanic's tool box? How when they glance

at their unmarked van with tinted windows?
When they make a mental
note, and the Dumpster there

half filled with debris, i.e., filled
just enough? I brushed some dirt away
from my face just this morning. I can stay up

all night with the nightmares I make for myself.
I wish I could teach myself to be less generous
in this fashion. Fortunately, Lonely Animal,

I am always alone when I begin to cry,
that the other animals will not see
the wound in me. Like gangrene

from a bear trap injury!
How it can't be carved out
with any knife I've sharpened,

and even fragrance, a lavender essence
poured over my temples, does nothing
to restore, but like I drowned

in breathing soft pulsing petals
and the pain beating there in the dark—
Oh Animal, the sun is falling over me now.

The sun, with all its dumb rectangles of light.
The sun, with its big broad shapes of light
yellow as dying catalpa leaves.

Dear Lonely Animal,

Last night I wanted nachos again,
a big plate of nachos covered in
cheese and black beans and

salsa, sour cream, guacamole—
did I mention cheese?
Animal, sometimes I want

nachos so much that it distracts me
from what I should be doing,
I mean, pursuing, I mean,

my career. How can one person's stomach
be so hungry for snacks?
It was Easter today and the local café

hid adhesive eggs under some people's
plates. I found an egg, but it
belonged to somebody else. People

were putting their plates in the dirty bin
without so much as a glance underneath!
Hel-lo!, I wanted to say, There's an egg hunt

in progress here, People! Later at a buffet,
different people put their drinks
on top of a grand piano—on the body

of a grand piano!—and their paper plates too
of crummy, half-eaten hors d'oeuvres!
Hel-LO!! Don't they know

how amazing a piano is?
What if somebody built that piano
with his bare hands

and lined up every hammer
and every key and every
damper and stretched

every single wire and tethered each one
in place? Somebody made that piano,
Lonely Animal, and its beautiful

wood-encased body, all arched and
elegant, a whole piece of wood
swooned into shape like that,

persuaded to the curve. And anyway,
I'm so stupid and scared. I didn't say
a word. I just let those people

put their soggy old plates
right on the instrument
and their sodas too, condensing

right on the wood, everybody laughing
and carrying on, not even
seeing it there, what it once was.

Like a coward, I came back
at ten o'clock at night, when the whole house
was empty except for me and the piano,

and I apologized to it. I opened up
its keyboard cover and the keys were
chipped and dirty, and the strings

were out of tune. I opened up the lid
and its body was filled with dust and even
a gum wrapper. Lonely Animal, I played then

the most beautiful piece of music
that I know, right there with all those
sour notes. The most beautiful

piece I know is the third movement
of Chopin's 3rd sonata. That's
a lot of 3's, but on repeating numbers,

you sometimes get to make a wish.
I didn't know what to wish for, but anyway,
I hope somebody somewhere made a wish.

Dear Lonely Animal,

I miss you. The other animals
are looking at porn again.
I will never dress or disrobe

in front of the other animals
ever again. Skin is different
than that. Bodies are different;

they're filled with eternity.
They exude rapture and light. Lonely
Animal, the other animals

are wearing black masks and
storming the press room toting
heavy weaponry and strapped with

belts of ammunition. The other
animals sport flouncy hair extensions.
They are taking each other on cruises

with that kind of caviar I can never
remember how to call.
The other animals are text-

messaging one another. I'm writing
to you, Lonely Animal. I will
never be a part of this world.

I should have built a
long-ago tower and lived there.
I've made mistakes, thinking

I found another animal
with whom I belonged. But
now where should I live?

Should it be the old factory
filled with broken glass?
I could manufacture tears

for the world and make
a million bucks. Jeweled
silver tears, crystal tears,

adhesive tears to gem to the face.
Beautiful long tears like
liquid metal cooled. So slender,

exquisite. Animal, there is a puddle
I love to step in: Splash!
The other animals talk so

important and stuff. I make
the cat and the sheep and the
pig sounds. I'm sad and I

make the sounds like the snail
and sometimes the clam. At least
the snail carries his home on his back.

If you put a snail down in a huge, wild
meadow filled with thistle and lace and clover,
insects, snakes, and mice, what are the chances

that that snail will find another snail
during his lifetime in all that terrain?
Even if two snails meet, what would they do?

I saw a documentary where the two snails
met and just mated right away.
They're all the same; everybody.

Dear Lonely Animal,

Let's have a collection competition:
I'll bet you have key chains, coins, sea shells,
stickers, postcards, stamps, photograph albums,

stacks and stacks of books, matchbox cars,
baseball cards, stuffed animals, CDs, DVDs,
those old Atari games, those old

Nintendo games, board games, puzzles,
mix tapes from long-ago lovers, letters
from erstwhile penpals, sketch books, notebooks,

diaries, garage sale vinyl records, ash trays,
mugs, National Geographic magazines,
Austrian crystal figurines, refrigerator magnets

of the U.S. states, probably some enormous jar
of buttons, probably wind-up toys and decks
of playing cards from places like

Niagara Falls, maybe even luggage locks and keys,
magic tricks, maybe lost/pulled/impounded teeth
hidden in a trophy in a row of trophies. Medals and

ribbons from the athletic tournaments,
bake-offs, and the farmhouse pageants. T-shirts
from the varied places. Corked bottles

of colored sand and flasks of essence, maybe
basketfuls of hotel soaps, shampoos, and lotions.
Maybe music boxes waiting to be wound—

But do you have shelves of chosen
rocks and pebbles, certain shapely twigs?
Pieces of broken porcelain, sea glass, scraps

of fabric from the different summer dresses?
Countless hand-dyed, blown-out eggs
and safety pins with plastic beads? Single earrings?

Torn sheets of handmade paper? Satin ribbons
and the folded wrappings of old presents? Calendars
from every year with scribbled details crowding

all the squares and margins? Autumn leaves
laid out on table surfaces, pressed beneath
discarded panes of glass? A stack of

rug samples to arrange in trails for leaping?
Star charts, empty jars and bottles, microscopic
slides and brine solutions, crystal-growing

kits and Sun Print paper, almost finished
latchhook grids, and sorted UPC symbols
saved from Kellogg's boxes— Have you

dipped your bandaged paws
in the river where you spread
your father's ashes?

Have you crouched alone
on piers to watch the crab-shapes
quiver underwater? Have you caught them

in a silver net to whisper words
and let them go again? Animal,
don't look at me with those eyes.

I can see from here the look
you are giving me as you read
this letter. You should know

this competition is not about eyes,
anyone could tell you that.
All our eyes with the near-transparent

callouses grown over them,
the nictitating membranes
sealing the other out. Dear Animal,

is that your paw print
here by my doorstep?
I looked for you this morning

in the snow, I thought perhaps you'd
come to find me, to be
together here, but everybody kept

trampling the tender damp
depressions, bristling by
with headphones on—

Dear Lonely Animal,

Sometimes I could just
burst into tears. I found some friends,
but they don't understand

I just don't care about baseball
and cupcake bakes and
beer pong. And I don't "hang out."

I don't like hanging out.
And I don't like bowling.
Sometimes I get in these moods, Animal,

and I become intolerable even to myself.
But I become very anxious
about my brain cells.

I feel that I need
all the brain cells I have.
Because I need to remember all the things

I saw and heard, and I need to remember
all the things I memorized.
And mostly all the people, especially

the people whom I miss the most.
I need to remember their voices and faces,
their real faces talking and laughing and not

some face from a photograph of them.
It's like all the real faces, when they're
gone for a while, they always

tend toward those photo faces and then
they become the photo faces and then I know
I've forgotten. And I could just bury myself

in the ground! I could just burst
into a million tears, sharp tears
like daggers that turn back on my body

and stab, stab, stab—tiny piercings
like tiny mouths biting all at once.
Like that Canadian goose somebody found

sitting by the side of the road, just
sitting there. Somebody lifted up
that huge bird and brought it in to us

at the Bird Rescue. The goose didn't
so much as honk or give even the slightest
whisper of a honk. It didn't

flap its wings or snap at anybody with its beak.
It looked tired, Lonely Animal.
Very tired. My aunt extended

one of the goose's wings to see
if the wing was broken
and there, under the wing, in the dense

body of the bird, was an injury
where some car or other
had hit it and driven away.

And in the injury there were
scores of maggots, teeming there,
boring into its soft body, devouring it

alive, mouthful by mouthful
with their tiny, smacking
maggot lips. You know that sound

maggots make when they're eating,
and mealworms too. A tiny wet smacking
like that gross sound when you stir up

macaroni and cheese. I have one friend
who does a great maggot impression.
But mostly my friends go on big

road trips and have dinner parties.
They talk about NPR. They ask me if I read
Billy Collins. NO I DO NOT

READ BILLY COLLINS. And anyway,
how can they forget their work like that?
Walking down the street with me,

one friend yelled "Fuck you"
at a stranger because he drove by
in a Hummer. Well, I hate all this

political bullshit and I could just
cry a million billion tears but what
good would it do? If one person

does not know how to treat
one other person, what good
are my million tears then?

Dear Lonely Animal,

I'm writing to you from the loneliest, most
secluded island in the world. I mean,
the farthest away place from anything else.

There are so many fruits here growing on trees
or on vines that wrap and wrap. Fruits
like I've never seen except the bananas.

All night the abandoned dogs howled.
I wonder if one dog gives the first howl, and if
they take turns who's first like carrying

the flag in school. Carrying the flag
way out in front and the others
following along behind in two long lines,

pairs holding hands. Also the roosters here crow
from 4 A.M. onward. They're still crowing right now
and it's almost noon here on the island.

Noon stares back no matter where you are.
Today I'm going to hike to the extinct volcano
and balance on the rim of the crater. Yesterday

a gust almost blew me inside. I heard
that the black widows live inside the volcano
far down below in the high grasses that you can't

see from the rim. Well, I was going to tell you
that this morning the bells rang and I
followed them and at the source of the bells,

there I found so many animals
all gathered together in a room
with carved wooden statues

and wooden benches and low wooden slats
for kneeling. And the animals were there
singing together, all their voices singing,

with big strong voices rising from even
the filthiest animals. I mean, I've seen animals
come together and sing before, except in

high fancy vaults where bits of colored glass
are pieced together into stories. Some days
I want to sing with them.

I wish more animals sang together all the time.
But then I can't sing sometimes
because I think of the news that happens

when the animals stop singing.
And then I think of all the medications
and their side effects that are advertised

between the pieces of news. And then I think
of all the money the drug companies spent
to videotape their photogenic, well-groomed animals,

and all the money they spent to buy
a prime-time spot, and I think, what money
buys the news, and what news

creates the drugs, and what
drugs control the animals, and I get so
choked I can't sing anymore, Lonely Animal.

I can't sing with the other animals. Because it's
hard to know what an animal will do when it
stops singing. It's complicated, you know, it's just

complicated—

IV

Text Message

oni, u rancorous scam, u r no rare ace.
no common sense. no sure win.
no amour. no sex. no career.
no suave swimwear, size six.
no amazonian eminence.
no renaissance in consciousness.
mere ire over asinine nuance.
u r so mesozoic era.

u rinse romaine + secure onions.
u use sour cream on venison.
u season noxious wieners.
coarse carnivore, u even wean + crisco sows
+ worse, simmer simian viscera
+ savor maximum cinnamon.
moreover, u evince ruinous manners.

ever since u came,
nauseous raccoons swoon + swerve near cars in manassas, va.
immense moose rave averse in maine.
monas wince in cameroon + zaire.
caimans careen in irreverence in so. american rivers.
nice vicunas amaze in serious cusses.
ewe emissions serve as severe consensus.
vermin vow never near.
even sea anemones voice censure.
wrens, vireos, caracaras, anis, emus, swans, macaws, canaries + cranes
maroon u, swear avian au revoir.
messiaen concurs.
eminem weaves mean verses on u.

o, oni, scorn us now,
now ur careworn carcass awes us.
a carrion-crow carves ur cameo, no
novocaine. incisive. immune.
nerve minus nerve is zero, or
noose, noon, nirvana: an
oceanic oasis. a rearview mirror.
can u recover now, oni?
can u crown ur cranium now,
can u rise in ur worm ascension?

we are ur vice, ur versus, ur
vice-versa, ur mesmeric new avarice,
ur concussion, ur amnesia (a caesura is u now, oni.)
(a caesura is ur new maison, ur caisson casa.)
we are ur arsenic, ur assassin,
ur anemia, ur anorexia nervosa.
we consume u, corrosive. we assess u.
we are ur vision, ur rescue mission, ur anima,
u. we use u. ur winsome camera crew:

coroner, commence exam, + camera man, zoom in:
a waxen woman, wear-worse.
corneas, ears + nose aswarm.
some recession on cranium.
venomous incisors, enormous.
varicose veins.
cursive arms over cavernous core.
nurse: scissors, ammonia.
carve in, coroner: mince, examine:
carmine amnion. uranium in urine.
in marrow, one amino amiss.

The Practice

Last night the moon followed me home
big and red and low, like a wounded ox.
It dragged itself after me with stertorous breathing.
It called names aloud hoping it would find my name in time.

Later, in my sleep, a girl had Pretty Poison, it was called.
A girl and her dog poisoned the entire village.
As a woman's face blossomed into sores, I heard her shout
Leave me alone, clawing animal. I can hear you

dying at the screen door. Don't look at me.
Don't come close to me. Get away from me.
"At least I have you to talk to, invisible friend,"
I said to no one as I woke in the pitch.

In my next dream, I killed a truly rotten individual I once had known.
I entered his room as he lay propped up in his invalid's bed
and I slit his back open with a fishing knife.
I emptied out his body like a laundry sack, like a complicated

wineskin, like a pig bladder, and then, that no one would notice
he was gone, that no one would find his skin, I stepped
into it and pulled it over me. Its gory warmth encased me,
rotting, decomposing around my own arms and legs and chest.

My face was covered with his puffy face, and my cheeks
began to mottle with rot, the skin purpling and flaking
as the day wore on. I kissed my husband with the dead man's face
over my face. *Forgive me*, I said in my dream.

And now, the loud light comes blaring through the light hatch.
Downstairs, I pass the plants struggling in dry soil.
The dust is languishing, perpetuating
on the living room shelves, on the tops of books, hundreds

of purchased, alphabetized books, chronological within author.
In the piano studio, the humidifier puffs its mist into the air.
Rainbows shoot in sun rays from a crystal on the window
and burst on the white walls. I step through some rainbows.

Some show on my t-shirt and some on my skin, like beauty
I like to think. I love it here, in the sunny room with rainbows.
Like birds flying on the walls. I love the sound
when it first enters the air, and how to shape the sound

lovingly like a glassblower shapes his molten glass, the loose
liquid molecules. I check the time and record the digits.
I sit on the bench. I wring my hands. I untangle my hands.
I lay them on the keys. So it begins, the practice.

That's Enough, Mr. Butterfly

The tortures have been enough today, Mr. Butterfly.
The sores are opening on my skin.
I feel a bulging beneath, a horrible
bloating of the glands and vessels,
a stretching taut of the muscular tissues.
Oh rusted-out vehicular body.
Pig-gut blown for a ball.

When he asked if I had standards,
I thought he meant
like golden candlesticks.
The tiny perfume bottles
arranged on their silver tray, here
by the mirror, here by the cracked
painting of the owl. The lotions
in descending order by size, by
shape of packaging, the
superficial reckoning of place.

For I must apply the salve
to produce the new skin at the rate
the old skin is falling off.
Though I could scrape the skin off faster.
Look at me!, I shout clawing to the Listeners.
Look!, I shout to the Lookers.
I'm a tiger!! I'm a she-wolf!
I'm a nanny-goat!
Oh, tiny ladybird beetle, you're not
as nice a beetle as people
think you are.

Outside, the church bells parcel
the wait: each hour tolls bright,
then drags its cape behind.
Or each hour, on the hour,
a new beaker smashed, the interim minutes
the languid ooze bent to press
its widening chemical burn, its
unstoppable circumference—
Or when the hour snaps open
like a magician's bouquet:
fresh flowers on a fresh
grave. Empty into me, the hour says.
Empty, says the hour.
And the gaping that remains, for what is it

I contain within, exactly?
I pull the pulp from sores
while more sores blossom. Soon,
my face—the indistinguishable tears
burning as they slide from one cavity
to another, electric body of sockets—

Oh, damselfly!
The leaves are of so many colors, like a sunburst!
Oh damselfly!
The pond is so wet this afternoon!
The grass has grown so high! Each blade waves
like a tall flexible tower! Each blade bends
like a flaccid slingshot! Each whistles
like an invisible
street urchin, like the wind
roped through excavated chambers,
a desiccated nautilus strung
with filaments of gold— Damselfly, is it
coiling or unraveling?
So many spheres, are the suns being born?

The Return

A man—from the snowy corridor
of a mountain of pines, from the heart
of that wilderness—a man

walks toward me. And the ravens fly out
from behind him. He has disturbed their roost,
their silent motionless perch and now they rage

past him like a funnel widening out,
cawing, beating their wings, a deafening funnel of black, he
at its center, walking toward me.

He has come back for me. He calls my name
through the hole in his throat. His head is held on
by a white bandage knotted tightly about the wound.

After the birds subside, he unbuttons
his filthy tartan shirt. With both hands,
he grasps his sternum and wrenches, by the bone,

his chest open like a glass cabinet before me.
For a second, nothing happens. I look in,
holding up my miniature binoculars.

I want to see the menagerie of animals I had
put there, so many beautiful animals
painted with the finest brush tips,

down to a single horse hair flecked
with a bead of paint: Winsor green,
cadmium yellow, manganese violet,

quinacridone rose red deep— The animals themselves
of glass and clay and jade and pewter.
Wood and china.

Some blown while liquid, some sculpted out from
their blocked materials, some dug up from the earth,
and one I found on the wooded path—

And from his chest, instead,
from its deep center, first
the raucous cries roused from sleep, then

the beating of wings, like the whole earth
quaked against me, and then the ravens pouring
outward from the source.

What do you want, I ask.

Are more ravens in those ravens' hearts?

A Hood Is Like an Ancient Chalice

A hood is like an ancient chalice
filled with another time, a time
before I was born, a quiet
time in which my
head can sleep, eyes
sinking back into the black
cavity, eyes setting further
and further beneath
the horizon, below the rim
of manmade lights, cool,
untethered from their stems

A hood is like a pristine puddle
in which my head can loosen
its stripped bolts, and the water
around my loosened head
seeps in through the cranial plates
and meanders through the
crevices of my brain, prying
in its course the dirty matter
from the coils. All the dirt
in my brain floats way up, away,
to the surface of the puddle,
and the dense matter sinks,
my skull, and the intelligent matter
is like electricity. When I think,
my brain electrocutes itself
inside the puddle of my hood

A hood is like a maroon canoe
and the head inside it like a body
lying long in the canoe—the body in the hull,

and around the hull, the water,
and around the hull,
the lull, so the body cradled
in the timeless hem of water, the body
sewn underwater in a pocket opening upwards,
and breathing from that pocket—
And the sky too pours out from the pocket,
erupts in blue, as if the body
from its ticking chest was gashed
and from the fissure, ribbons flew,
blue ribbons streaming out
like daylight kites to merge and blur—
The descending eye glimpses
from its rocking casket, just
observation, no recognition, no
memory of sky, but a pure witnessing of
satin rupture from the painless
heart of some more objective
self, some assemblage
of matter, floating matter of
undetermined density equivalent
to the water it displaced

Maroon Canoe

o canoe, maroon canoe
over mesmeric waves we row
over an azure ionian sea
over mariners' mum communion
over icarus's un-ascension
over men-o'-war + runner missions
over ice-run ruins, over anxious cruises
over seismic omens + vesuvian ooze
we row, we row
ravenous sea, reassure me
reserve me an amnesia, caesura,
a serene unconscious ease

o canoe, maroon canoe
we row in seven rains + six monsoons
we row in summer snows
seven seasons wax + wane
we row near sorceress circe's manor
(six + seven swine nurse acorns, en masse aware)
we row near sirens + swoon severe
(voices immerse us, caress our ears in razor arias),
we row near mermen, oceanic emissaries on a wave
our oars announce us in murmur, in susurrous music
sonorous sea, connoisseur in snare: un-accuse, excuse me
aeonic erosion, receive me, examine + rewire
cure me + rename

a carmine sun commences an aurora, an amorous soiree
one moon arc answers in romance
orion rises + canis minor carves noir
a near aroma—some essence, some evanescence—
arouses in me remorse + reminiscence:

some once omission, some non-reunion, some
mirror version, some overcome
evasion, a misnomer, a woe, a sorrow— o canoe,
maroon canoe, o sea swerve, o
ceremonious casanova,
o crimson sea serene,
unweave our sinuous maze, our nexus
renew me, new—no
secrecies, evasion—
a sum immersion in a now

o raw maria on moon, o unison sun,
o universe worn in unconcern,
issue a summons, convene + reconvene
+ answer me
is a souvenir a sorrow sewn
are cocoons meaner secrecies
is erasure a crime
is reverence so rare
is an error ever overcome

soon, maroon canoe; soon, reservoir severe:
a missive scriven in cruor, in rime

Today Mr. Rufo

Today Mr. Rufo died. During a game of bocce ball,
he leaned on his friend's shoulder and died.
Just five minutes before we found out, Jon and I
had been walking with our dumb, bourgeois fruit smoothies,
and we stopped by a bush that had all these purple flowers
bursting out of it, and I said, Look how the dead flowers
are a darker purple, a bluish blackish purple
and the live flowers are magenta. Do you think
the dead flowers used to be magenta, or did all
the darker purple flowers die first?
(The dead flowers crumpled closed like soggy
paper umbrellas, while the live ones stretched open, each
like a child's hand reaching—)

Afterwards, all the family came and assembled and
sat outside together on the patio. For days, I did not see
Mrs. Rufo. She must have been inside the house
all that time. Meanwhile a big yellow garden spider
built his web above the plot of dirt and weeds
and wildish plants that's just beside their outside staircase.
It's true that spiders are noiseless, I realized,
watching the spider in its nonstop industry, listening to the spider.
All of us have read "A noiseless, patient spider…"
but to hear, really, that absence of sound
is something altogether different. Because the soundlessness
is transparent and shaped like a geometric plane.
It casts a silent white shadow that's bigger
than the spider is big, and when the spider dies,
the silence that replaces its silence
is bigger than the spider's silence was big.

The Bells

The bells for the hours have not been ringing lately.
It's been weeks since I heard them, but only a day
since I noticed, suddenly, that extended absence, that blank
stretching backwards through the month like a long,

lustreless carpet I had already been walking, mindless
with my own humming. Jon thinks perhaps
some mechanical thing has gone wrong in the tower.
The roof underneath is continually in shambles. The yard

is filled with scrap debris among which anonymous people
sometimes rake. The oversized terra cotta pots brim
with dead marigolds. Perhaps someone will launch a campaign
to raise money to repair the bells, so all of us can know again

just how much time has passed, how many hours
we have squandered, and how many we still have left,
God willing, to make up for it. Meanwhile,
a baby bird fell from somewhere high,

and died against the silver cargo wall
of Jon's pickup truck. Its body remained stuck there,
its tiny immature wings splayed out, its reptilian skin, its swollen
blue eyes with transparent lids slit over the bulging.

One day when I came to the truck, all
that was left of the bird was its skeleton
and some membrane webbing the bones— The bones:
exquisitely thin and perfectly placed, like an ancient

imported lace from the holds of some incredible
vessel, Roman corbita filled with silks and gems and spices—
I wish I knew how much time it had taken
for the body to reach this stage of arrangement.

Then one day at the truck, just a few bones jutted
at odd divergent angles, a gutted castle. Later I came back
and all of the bird was gone. I didn't see it go. It must have
blown away while we were driving like so much dust.

Spring

This morning, I slammed my knee
against the bottom bed frame corner hidden by quilts.
I didn't know today would be the day
Robert Creeley died. Just stopped

breathing; they call that
"respiratory failure." I just saw him two weeks ago
having a sense of humor about the deterioration
of the body. He said you wake into awe again

after age 50, like a baby wakes into awe,
or like a teenager waking daily into his dizzying,
unfathomable development. And at age 50,
again, because parts you never knew you had

suddenly make themselves known in their
malfunction, in their arbitrary collapse.
It's so sunny today that I went outside
to walk around a bit. I don't want

my teachers to die. The world is so
stupid without them, obstinate and stupid.
I walked past the big vans that load and unload
their gaudy, awful furniture,

opening their big blue rear doors and
slamming them shut again. One of the vans
had somebody's matted sweatshirt peeling
off the back of the driver's seat. When I looked

on the pavement behind the van, I saw
a sparrow that the van had run over. The sparrow
was completely flattened with its wings splayed out.
The church bells rang right then. Either it was three o'clock,

or the bird was three years old, like how
they used to ring the number of years a person lived
at his funeral. I don't want to go home again
so quickly, but it's not as warm out here as I thought.

In fact, it's cold out here. The sun
is white and cold after all. And anyway, the trash is blowing.
That blind man that lives at the top of the hill
is feeling his way up the hill again from the street below.

Now his right hand is on the telephone pole and his left
is flitting his white cane back and forth. I run by him
as quietly as I can. My landlady's dead Christmas tree
is out in the rubbish heap. I guess it's spring.

V

The Mandrake Vehicles

NOTE ON THE MANDRAKE FORM

Paper version:

The following pages contain the physical version of three kinetic poems called the Mandrake Vehicles, scored for paper, letters, and imagination, each vehicle represented here by seven stilled frames selected from the vehicle that itself is in constant motion. Each of the three vehicles begins with a large text block concerning the biological development, folklore, occult ritual, magical association, and medicinal/homeopathic usages of the mandrake plant (sometimes spoken in the voices of the plants themselves). In selecting material for the Mandrake Vehicles, I conflated some of the more famous occult associations of the European mandrake with the biological structure and development of (as well as the many diverse associations and medicinal uses relating to) the American mandrake, also known as the mayapple. Both the European and American mandrakes have a rhizomatous root structure, meaning that the plants themselves are all connected underground by horizontal subterranean stems shooting off from the vertical root of each individual plant. This rhizomatous characteristic of the plants gave rise to the layered, interconnected form of the Mandrake Vehicles.

Formally, all three vehicles are connected by their surface layers, as the large text blocks that begin each of the vehicles can themselves be read continuously from one text block to the next (in their consecutive order). However, each text block also conceals a depth of two additional "secret" poems that can be distilled from the top layer (these inner poems appear in their solidified forms on pages 4 and 7 of each vehicle). In each vehicle, both of these inner poems have technically been visible all along in the top layer, but their embedded letters remain undetected because of the presence of the other letters and characters. Each embedded poem becomes revealed as the "lighter" letters float off the surface of the vehicle and the "heavier" letters remain anchored on the page (the grids of heavier letters that remain after the lighter letters lift off are shown on pages 2 and 5 of each vehicle). The remaining heavier letters eventually solidify into one of the two inner poems, forming new words, new contexts, and new patterns of sound, structure, and meaning, while still maintaining the order in which they appeared in the initial text block. In addition to the new and sometimes parallel relationships created between the contents of the three poems of each vehicle, relationships are also forged between words of the different layers that share the same letter(s). The trajectory of a letter can be traced by following the words it helps to form, and necessarily the relationship of these words to one another must then be considered, as residue of meaning is carried by the letter as it moves from one word to the next.

Finally, pages 3 and 6 of each Mandrake Vehicle depict stilled shots of the "liquid" layers contained in each of the vehicles. These are the pages on which the reader witnesses the remaining grids of heavier letters in the moments just after the lighter letters have unmoored and floated away. The remaining letters are then in transitional states, loose states of organization in which their spacing no longer functions to delineate one word from another, and there is no punctuation to regulate words into grammatical units. In these unstable "liquid" layers, the letters function by fluctuating through the spaces that surround them toward the letters nearest to them in their loose grid (one must imagine the constant atomic movement that is present on this very oversimplified printed page). Letters move horizontally, attracted to the letters on either side of them, forming multiple words simultaneously. In addition, the letters in the liquid layers begin to shed scales of themselves. While the letters themselves stay in their grid space, their shed scales fall down the page vertically, colliding with other scales and eventually forming detritus words which accumulate in a heap at the bottom of the page (again, the page functions as a stilled snapshot of a continuing process, and one can imagine the parade of detritus words continuing to fall well after the snapshot has been taken). The detritus words are the trash cast off by the process, and are never used anywhere in any of the three vehicles. They are made of scales (or shadows) of the same heavy letters that will form the next poem, but they create "could-have-been" words which exist

only as unselected entities, and they evaporate from the vehicle during the next page turn. When the letter grid of a liquid layer solidifies, becoming pressed together horizontally (complete with added punctuation and word groupings), one of the embedded poems now becomes visible, having cooled into its shape. At this point, either the process begins again or the core poem of the vehicle has been reached.

Flash animation:

This computerized version of the Mandrake Vehicles, expertly Flash-animated by the incomparable Betsy Stone Mazzoleni and placed on an autorun Flash CD enclosed inside the back cover of this book, makes most of the motions of my invented Mandrake form immediately comprehensible. Now visible are the letter lift-offs, the scale-shedding of unstable letters in the liquid layers, the collision of the scales in their descent down the face of the poem, the accumulation of the detritus words, the solidifying of liquid texts into legible inner poems, and—in this case, only represented in the animated version—a color narrative of the plant's (and of the poem's) ripening as the reader progresses through all three vehicles.

The Flash animation, although enormous in the scope of its accomplishments, has its limits as well, and the boundaries of its abilities are themselves interesting to compare to the "ideal" (undocumented) state of the Mandrake Vehicles. Most notably, in the rendering of the Flash animation, Betsy and I were not able to portray the randomness and individuality that is written into the paper version of the poems because of the decisions she necessarily had to make about where each letter would physically be placed along the timeline of the animation, decisions which are remade exactly each time the animation is played. In the paper version, because of the enormous blank spaces between the frames, and the work that each individual reader has to accomplish to fill these spaces with text motions of his/her own imagining, the individual text motions of the vehicles become vastly different not only from one reader to the next, but every time any given reader re-encounters the work. No two people will replicate in their imaginations the exact manner or the exact order in which the lighter letters unmoor from a poem and float away, or how a letter in the liquid layer puffs off or possibly oozes or accidentally drops a scale of itself, or the manner in which that scale tumbles down the page and collides with other scales in its descent, or exactly how and in what order the jumble of detritus words accumulates in a heap at the bottom of the page, or how slowly or quickly, how smoothly or sporadically a liquid layer presses together to solidify into the next poem. Also notably, in the Flash animation, Betsy and I sacrificed (for the purpose of clarity in the animation) the constant horizontal attractions of letters in the liquid layer to nearby letters in their environment. For example, in any imagining of the "ideal" Mandrake version, the letters "s h   o   verti ll   " within the fourth line of the very first liquid layer, as they fluctuate from side to side could read "shove," "HOV," "hover," "over," "overt," "vert," "till," "ill," and "I'll" nearly simultaneously. These same letters could be attracted to letters in adjacent

lines and form even more words, not to mention suggesting by their approximations dozens of others.

Although the Flash animation has its several mechanical limitations, it overwhelmingly exists as a powerful and accurate depiction of the heart and workings of the Mandrake Vehicles, and I am astounded and profoundly humbled to have this documented animation of Betsy Stone Mazzoleni's individual, human encounter with the letters. Although I designed all of the text motions, it was Betsy who, as the actual animator, envisioned the specifics of all the letters' motions throughout the animation, and her personality and individuality shine through in all her renderings, most notably her humor (and intense craftsmanship) in liquid layer detritus words such as "cartoon," "helium," "drool," "oriflamme," "montage," "fatso," "Cyclops," "dumpling," and many others which I am still, to my incredulous and grateful amazement, noticing and discovering, though I have watched this animation hundreds of times. I could not have remotely dreamed of such a fantastic consciousness giving so much of itself to the letters, words, motions of this poem.

N.B.

The American mandrake plant is one of the first plants to come up in spring, transforming the barren destruction of winter on the forest landscape into a broad cloth of thriving green. March 20, the usual date of the vernal equinox in the Northern Hemisphere, also marks the beginning of the Iraq War. Early in the morning on March 20, 2003, the first U.S. cruise missiles hit Baghdad.

not knowing enough to shriek when (not knowing when) they were pulled, a root hair, when the tendrils broken, the network of unfurling towards, and the long lines connecting them underground (oh at first they had only grown vertically from the dirt, a mere), at first the piercing (a thin shriek as the stem passed through the rub—the dull catch at the cylindrical surround, of the follicles against the grainy remnants) (or a shrill?—eternal, as the metal axis pushed timeless through the iron heart of the earth)—was it—of surface, liminal, for first there was a layer, *first*, a membrane of dust to host the infinitesimal rupture (the shed skins loosed to granule)—*(and the shedder of skins, first?)*, the upheaval of plane from below, as from a slow lymphatic magma congregating its massive but disparate angers—call it desire—and the stem emerging, *forth*, and the volume of sky in blue, like a cellophane to enfold in sheer the arriving, to laminate the pushing blade, the shape as ever its confines reach (a hope), as ever, from all sides hearing the loved voice, warm, it sends out ears to the vast dome, emissaries of devotion, though ever the song a liquid of tongues, the slim words dissolving, though ever the pulsing source a fainter circle, distant insignia, and *beyond* (though the enraptured green makes a fluttering of lashes, the grounded one pleading [*again?*])—but the brighter thing like on the other side of glass, a passing in arc—And is it not enough to see (though still the great blue insulation enwraps, a tangible between, a fibrous), still—still the tiny peering from beneath the blunt rock as beyond, the beautiful pale curve [as a cheek] subsides, a mask-shard declined from a far dark face—and *still* the eventual banners urged from the earth, wrung from the earth (as tears, as a gratefulness born withering), end (*begin?*) unfurling green in the blue day, in the white day, umbrellas for the patio of dirt awaiting—and in the meantime (an unmarked *always* segmented by the turned and overturned sand) the dirt agreeing on points from the typed agenda, a construct in dots

t   owing no gh o s   t nowing   the
we   ll d a r t air   en t   e   r s b   en t   ne wor
      f ling   s a   lo   nes c   e   n   t
underg   n   at s h   o   verti ll
the dir   er   a f   t   r ing a   sh e   s h   em
pas   t rough   e r   h   ull a   t   ri al
     r un   of he   ll   s aga   e   r   r   ant
h il   t   al as t me al   s p   ed   les t   the
      n ear   t ear h   it   s face m   a   r   s
the   w   ay *fir*   em   ust   host the
n in es   u ture   d   n oose o   r   le   *a d*
the s e   r o s ins   st   e   p a   pl   om b
as   m a l   l   hat   a co r   n i s   a ve
   is a t anger   i   n   e   m   i   *rth*
a   he   l m of s y   c ophan t   d in
s ee he ar in to min e   pu   l   s   e as
     it conf e reach   h   e a   ve f   al s e   aring
he l   d vo   w   t end   e r to h   ast   e
miss   e   d voti   ve h   id
to gues   sl   or   d s l ing   e r t   u   g
ource   nter i c e   s a   sign   a *be nd* t o
n a ture   ree   k s a lu te   as   t   ounded
ne   e ding   but he   ight   hing   e on   e
   h   id f a   ng   ar   d   en   t
see th   e   blu   n   t n e w   s a tan
bet   a   ti   the t y pe in fro   th
the lu   ck   y d   utiful p le   as   e
   u s de   a d   in   f o   r   ce   d
s l e eve   s r ed from he art   r   o   t
      as te rs   a   r ef l   o   w eri   n   *gin*
      li   th   u   a   n   i   a   b ell s
t e p i   d r awa n   d in t   e nt   n a ked
a wa s   ted   d a   r   e sa   t e d
ag e   s o   pe   nda   n tru   in   s

t   owing no gh o s   t nowing   the
we   ll d a r t air   en t e   r s b   en t   ne wor
      f ling   s a   lo   nes c   e   n t
underg   n   at s h   o   verti ll
the dir   er a f t   r ing a   sh e   s h   em
pas   t rough e r   h ull a   t   ri al
     r un of he ll s aga   e r   r   ant
h il   t al as t me al   s p ed   les t   the
     n ear   t ear h   it   s face m   a   r s
the w   ay *fir*   em   ust   host the
n in es   u ture   d n oose o r   le   *a d*
the s e   r o s ins   st   e p a   pl   om b
as   m a l l   hat   a co r   n is a ve
is a t anger   i   n e m   i   *rth*
a   he l m of s y   c ophan t   d in
s ee he ar in to min e   pu   l   s e as
   it conf e reach h e a ve f   al s e   aring
he l d vo   w   t end   er to h ast   e
miss e   d voti   ve h   id
to gues   sl   or d s l ing   e r t   u g
ource   nter i c e s a   sign a *be nd* t o
n a ture ree   k s a lu te   as   t   ounded
ne e ding   but he ight hing e on e
h id f a   ng ar   d   en t
see th   e   blu n t n e w s a tan
bet a   ti   the t y pe in fro   th
the lu   ck   y d   utiful p le   as   e
u s de   a d   in f o r   ce   d
s l e eve   s r ed from he art r   o t
   as te rs a r ef l   o w eri   n *gin*
   li   th u a n   i a   b ell s
t e p i d r awa n   d in t e nt   n a ked
a wa s ted   d   r   e sa t e d
ag e   s o   pe   nda   n tru in s

tatters non-puce miner gastric antelope frenetic mongoose trellis Depacote
rilles orrery ballet oasis tryst astral typhoon hewn plangent sea nettles radishes
haunt askew tolling towel narc décor veered spite martian saints stave glissando
Ave Maria cosecant umiak lease seraphim invests winter rants tsar twit tarot
dicey straw victor gargle anemone ascent cogent mustard cartoon emanates hemoglobi

Towing no ghost, no wing, the
well-dart air-enters bent new or
flings a lone scent
under. Gnats hover, till
the dire raft-ring ashes' hem
past rougher hull, a trial
run of hell-saga, errant
hilt, a last meal sped lest the
near tear hits face, mars
the way— Fire must host the
nine-sutured noose, or lead
these rosins step aplomb.
A small hat, acorn, I save.
Is a tangerine mirth?
A helm of sycophant din?
See, hear into mine pulse as
it confer each heave false, a ring-
held vow tender to haste,
missed votive, hid
to guess lords linger, tug.
Our center ices: a sign. A bend to
nature reeks a lute astounded,
needing but height, hinge, one
hid fang, ardent—
Seethe, blunt new Satan:
bet a tithe, type in froth.
The lucky, dutiful please
us—dead, in forced
sleeves red from heart-rot.
Asters are flowering in
Lithuania, bells
tepid, raw, and intent. Naked,
a wasted dare sated
ages, o pendant ruins.

              win no   wing he
                  art   s   t   o
l   e   nt
und r   a s   o   r ti
                      ng   em
pa t   h   i
          e sag   r
                  e   e   th
      a t a   mar
t   y   r   st o
    ne   d   se   e d
      s   t   omb
      s al   t a   r   sav
Is   e in   t
A   c   t
              a   m   ul e
    t o   ch   a   f e a ri
        d   ste
m sse v   e
                  rd   i   r t g
        u   t   a g   e d t
      re e s   l   e st   ed
      e   n   b   e g   in
        a g arden
S   he   l
                  t   e   r
      he l   p ease
us   dea   f ced
        e   d from
        e   ar
        th   bel
te d   w an   te   d
          d   e a   d
        o pen   u   s

```
    win  no          wing  he
        art        s     t        o
l          e    nt
und r      a s   o  r ti
                ng        em
pa t      h            i
        e   sag    r
            e     e      th
    a  t a           mar
t      y    r     st  o
    ne        d    se    e d
    s        t     omb
    s  al    t  a  r    sav
Is      e in    t
A           c      t
        a      m    ul e
t  o        ch    a   f  e a ri
    d                    ste
m sse   v    e
            rd  i    r t g
    u    t        a  g        e d t
      re  e  s   l  e st      ed
    e   n  b    e g    in
      a  g arden
S   he   l
            t   e    r
    he l              p ease
us   dea     f  ced
        e    d from
        e   ar
    th      bel
te  d   w an   te        d
        d    e  a  d
        o pen       u  s
```

mouse irate Noah bane Wimbledon dehisce stress derelict tarantella
heathen sorrel dossier renegade Easter interest gem tinder rhombus friend estate
treacherous asinine restart banshee teems margin gestate wire deleted teaches
pantomime natal patent sanguine mail lunette atlas restorative barter folds lattice

Winnowing heart
(stolen tundra
sorting empathies),
agree that a
martyr stoned
seeds tombs, altars:
a vise intact.
A mule to chafe
arid stems,
sever dirt. Gut
aged trees
lest Eden begin
a garden shelter.
Help ease us:
deaf, ceded
from earth, belted,
wanted dead.
Open us—

while the outpour, while the spilling tenets of green, the green parting to merge again on the far side of trunks (the still throats cloaked, the cut throats shrouded— [a suggestion, as the webbed root, rhizomatic, ground fine by the pestle, powdered]), for so the young ones loved nothing, could be pulled mute from the earth (and the bluff, the far planets turned silent on their pins, a tethered chariot to drag the moon, dull nub of eraser)—(It: a great wind, It: the prowling approaches with the breath of berries, It: fewer legs, the digits leathered, It: stained, stained, a dull ringing [and as if from within a clouded depth of water, the deaf hearing their name called, the deaf turning toward their name, at last, as from an old life])—pulled, or by lever—for only the old ones could bear, and too the olders shrieked (a once and gone, for in the sever, we all cried out unknowing—all of us tied, and the pain—then silence, and one of us missing who must too have helpless called and none of us heard, having deafened our ears with what rose as if from another throat, as if the dirt yawned up, sobbing, and the sound unbidden covered him and now the taken gone and we not hearing again but waiting, hushed, and the warmth not close enough, never enough, and the bright seeming, *seaming*, an underfold), and so the left olders clung for the bearing, the single stem fractured, so from the broken: arms: one white flower, hung—(or by coil, by the head-weight dropped and the body, with beneath kicked away, and the catch absent: the buoyant, arms to break the falling—and the catch: a cold sticking of breath, crude halt in the pendulum), and so the olders waiting: each one alone holding its two umbrellas, and the born, the borne thing between, at the gap of seams, in the path of the falling—for no one could see it coming (at the petiole [tipped pedestal] a dropper) and the flower disheveled in a ruffle of white, deeply dyed, a clear distillation: clear on the still lip [for some of them drank], hardened on the hardened lip, as a fine glue of sky—

w   e   e   p   le the s lin   nets   gree   t
pa   ge a   n   t   s   of tru   th s
th   ats c   a   the cu   r   t s   o ded   ges
h   o   r izo   nd i   e   th   e
pow er   s h   oun   d   g   o ld
   le   t   o   th e   r   b uff   e   r   s
   r   e   lent o   r   n   a teth re   a   t   drag   on
du   n   e   ser   r a   n   t he ro in
     aches w   e   f   es   t   er le s the
le ther d   tain   t   ed   r   a d a   r
   thin   ou   r   d a   ring t   ame
all   d   ur ing   war   the r   e a l st a   r
     fe   ll d   r y l   o   o   t   e   d   co ld
b   oo t   l e s s   a   n   e   n   g   in   e
     we a   ried   owing   l   us t d an   t e
pain   t   s   a d o   o   m   ing ho   st
hel l s cal d   one   s h ard   a   n   d   en d   ur e
     hat   e a   m   other thr   as   he d r   aw
   so   ng a   h   idden   ver d   an   t
   en g   e   nd   e   ring   but   t   e   a
he   ar   th   lo   ver   no   n   ight
        n   a i   a   de   a   s   e   s
o   the   r   sing e st   c ure   s   o   the   r
ar   s on wh   ow r   ung   l   ight
   op e   n   the bo y   i   en   t   ic ed w   e
c   h   a   nt the b   ant a ms o   ra t e fa in   t
a ch   o   i   r   cru e   l in h   um
an   o th   ers wa n   e ch o   lo   o   ng i s t
   b ell s a d   orn the b r   i   bet ee   th
f   am   in   e   a   f   e   l   o   n   co ld s
o   ng a   h   ole ti   d   al   op er a
f   eve   r   e   d   p   e   a c e
   st ati   clea   n   s ill li   f   the   r
   arden   t   har   ne   s   s

w   e   e   p   le the s lin   nets   gree   t

pa   ge   n   t   s of tru   th s

th   ats c a   the cu   r   t s o ded   ges

h   o   r izo   nd i e   th   e

pow er   s h oun   d   g o ld

le   t   o   th e r   b uff   e   r   s

r e   lent o   r   n a teth re   a t   drag   on

du n   e ser   r a   n   t he ro in

aches w   e   f   es t   er le s the

le ther d   tain   t   ed   r   a d a   r

thin   ou   r   d a   ring t   ame

all   d   ur ing war the r   e a l st a r

fe   ll d r y l   o o   t e   d   co ld

b   oo t   l e s s   a n e n g   in e

we a   ried   owing   l   us t d an t e

pain t   s   a d o   o   m ing ho   st

hel l s cal d   one   s h ard a n d   en d ur e

hat   e a   m   other thr   as   he d r   aw

so   ng a   h   idden ver d   an   t

en g e nd e   ring   but   t   e   a

he   ar   th   lo   ver no   n   ight

n   a i   a   de   a   s   e   s

o the   r   sing e st   c ure s   o   the   r

ar s on wh   ow r   ung   l   ight

op e   n the bo y i   en t   ic ed w   e

c   h a   nt the b   ant a ms o r a t e fa in   t

a ch   o   i   r   cru e   l in h   um

an   o th   ers wa n   e ch o   lo   o   ng i s t

b ell s a d   orn the b r   i   bet ee   th

f am in e a   f e l   o n   co ld s

o   ng a h   ole ti   d al   op er a

f   eve   r   e   d p   e   a c e

st ati   clea   n   s ill li f   the   r

arden   t   har ne   s   s

pathetic gossamer dentist arboreal Zoroastrian garnish hobbit vacuous deet raccoon
pirée lectern banal montage Gethsemane oriflamme fedora cursory ballot drench walleye
helium geriatrics panther aleatoric scattergram Teflon mud dauber Geronimo
Neolithic séance drool zounds geranium threnody cuisine Dracula toddler Gestapo
newts patrician gosling stethoscope suet twill rebel flea bitten onager laudanum geode

Weep, Lethe's linnets, greet
pageants of truths
that scathe curt sod. Edges
horizon-die. The
powers hound gold,
let other buffers
relent. Ornate threat, dragon
dunes, errant hero—in
aches we fester, lest He
let herd-tainted radar
thin our daring tame.
All during war, the real star
fell dry, looted cold,
bootless. An engine
wearied, owing lust. Dante
paints a doom in ghost
hell. Scald one shard, and endure
hate: a mother thrashed raw.
(Song: a hidden verdant-
engendering butte, a
hearth-lover no night-
naiad eases.)
Others ingest cures (other:
arson who wrung light
open; the boy I enticed). We
chant; the bantams orate faint:
a choir cruel in hum,
another swan-echo, loon-gist.
Bells adorn the bribe. Teeth,
famine. A felon cold. (S-
ong: a hole. Tidal opera.)
Fevered Peace,
static, leans ill. Lift her,
ardent harness—

                    th   in
pa ean s   ru
        s   t   s   Edges
        z   i Th
      ers h un g
e   r   f
            Or at t   a   r
                a   hero in
        es we e t   s He
l t   er   ed
      in o r a ng   e
All   uring w   he e l sta
    ll   y   co d
        es   n   ine
w   i d ow   s   te
p i   d   host
        S al one hard   en   r
    ate   moth   s   d raw
    So   dden   ant
en n   a
    eart   ver   g
          e s
O   ngest ures o
ar on who   r
        e   b   ent
      ant he   ms o   f
a   n
a   r   ch   ist
        s   he r e T
        i   c   S
              ol   o
Fe   ce
sta i   n   t e
    de   ar

                    th   in
pa ean s   ru
        s t   s   Edges
        z   i Th
        ers h un g
  e   r   f
            Or at t   a   r
                a   hero in
        es we e t   s He
l t   er   ed
    in o   a ng   e
All   uring w   he e l sta
  ll   y   co d
          es   n   ine
  w   i d ow   s   te
  p i   d   host
        S al one hard   en   r
    ate   moth   s d raw
    So   dden   ant
en n   a
    eart   ver   g
            e s
  O   ngest ures o
  ar on who   r
      e   b   ent
    ant he   ms o   f
  a   n
  a   r   ch   ist
        s   he r e T
        i   c   S
            ol   o
  Fe   ce
  sta i   n   t e
    de   ar

Sri Racha swaddle infatuated tenuto pawpaw tree enigma niçoise henna grenade
remora cirrus triune greenhouse succor Hecate wrestle diorama tufted owl ghetto
trowel pewter rodeo wisteria hedonist tetrahedron itinerant étagère fatso scion ruthless
Grendel tufa integer damned EZ cheese sewer dressage thrawn estuary

Thin paeans rust
sedges. Zithers
hunger for attar:
a heroine sweet . . .
sheltered . . . in
orange alluring . . .
Wheels tally codes.
Nine widows,
tepid hosts, alone
harden, rate moths,
draw sodden
antennae: art
verges on gesture.
Soar on,
whore-bent anthems
of anarchists,
heretic solo,
feces-tainted ear.

for it promised sleep in delicate voice, for how must the blossom be discovered but sadness swayed a body to its knees, the bloom obscured by lonely parasols of green (for deeply, deeply the opposing lobes divided), and seen through the wet lash, sudden, like grace, a silent thing looks on in white, as if the heart's damp handkerchief rubbed gently through the casing, and hanging face-down offers *sleep*, a nauseating scent wafting from its yellow center where buffed trumpets herald in formation, a circle-lure for the liquid self [invisible, eternal the want] to pour, a tongue of light lisped in by fork, to pry dark molecules open—*for what's the lethal dose of us?*—delirium, by grief to drink the tincture or taste a shaving of the mortal stem, *for we yield a three percent of ash upon incineration, for we sway indifferent lovers who drink the philtres of our mix*, for rubbed externally, a burning, though the moon be full above the gallows tree, or infusion of the extract, or inhaled soporific vision [procession of the dead, the threaded animals who came when called, unknowing, tied about the excavated base and called by name, came running toward a loved, familiar voice]—*for we the first to rise, before the panoply of leaves, and we, arriving through the thaw, the urgent cloak of bones, we cover first the wreckage*—but then the swelling of the flower into sphere, which sometime in the ripening (from petulance to succulence) persuaded, and sometime blushed to yellow, fragrant—for all about, the sun, the air, the moss converged in steadfast deed, an easy warming of the basking leaves, a buoyancy of petal, a soft embracing of the fibers—and from the clenched green surface of the rind, worked inward to the center, from all sides inward, and found there a petal hiding, its dented crown in shambles, its anguish befuddled, and it: ripe for a new wondering—so swayed, the thin shafts of poison realign to nectar, the undone toxin ripe for the bee sip, to rosin the drawn legs of the grasshopper, varnish for the pulled note, a stay in slash against the slate—

        p o ised s   in deli   v   e   r   o   ust
blo om   s   red bu   d   s s   ed a   t   e
t   om bscure b   one   par   ol   en or   eply
   p y th o   n l   ivid   a d   rough   t
ash   udde   r ce a si n   g   s o i   w   as i
he   ar dam   an   ch e rubbe   nt y   ou   th
as   a d a g g   er   p a   us ing s ent
aft n   o   i s y low   n e where buffed tru   t h a   n
     i   ci cle   e   quid   i   s   t
      ant   p   r   ong   s   d i   r t   y
   r   ules ope   r   at   e   al o   of
deli m by   e t d i   ct   a te s aving
mor al s   w   ield a   p   ent   s   u   n
in i   r   on   or   sw   ind   l   e   w o   r   the
ph   e   m   e   r all   a u   g h
   e   on   l ove th   a   w t   or in s   e
ex   i   led p ri   s on   so   f   dea   th
t r ade a   s h   ame   c   un n   ing   ed
   u   ca ted ba   l d   me   n
   wa   ve fa   vo   r   the irst   ri   f e
t   oply   an   e   rri ng th ough t   tha   t
       oa   f   s   cove   t   r   age bu t
   swel   t   er   s here whi   t   e
     ing   o   t lance t   cu   rs   ed a
s   tim   u   l   ant f all   e   n
th   ir t e   e   n s adfa de d an e   w
        king   s   o   n   p l as t e   r
th   r   o   n   e   s face   the
wor   nward   enter ro   r   fo nd
th re a   t   di g its   d rown n   am es   a
b   and it   f   a   w   n e   yed
  hin   ts of poi   ign o   r   e   don t
f r   e   e   i   t   i   draw l s of t   as hop e
va nish   e   d no e as y   s a   gai t   slate

          p o ised s   in deli   v   e   r   o   ust
blo om   s   red bu   d   s s   ed a   t   e
t   om   bscure b   one   par ol   en   or   eply
     p y th o   n l   ivid   a d   rough   t
ash udde   r ce a si n   g   s o i w   as i
he   ar   dam   an   ch e   rubbe   nt y   ou   th
as   a d a g g   er   *p* a   us   ing s ent
aft n   o   i s y low   n e where buffed tru   t h a   n
      i   ci cle   e   quid   i   s   t
        ant   p r   ong   s d i   r   t   y
    r   ules ope   r   *at*   e   *al* o   *of*
deli   m by   e t d i   ct   a te s aving
mor al s   *w* *ield a*   *p* ent   s   u   n
in i   r   on   or   sw   ind   l   e w o r   the
ph   e   m   e   r all   a u   g h
  e   on   l   ove th   a w t   or in s   e
ex   i   led   p ri   s on   s o   f   dea th
t r ade   a   s h   ame   c   un n   ing   ed
    u   ca ted ba   l d   me   n
  wa   ve   fa   vo   r   *the irst   ri   f e*
t   oply   an   e   rri ng th ough t   tha   t
       oa   f   s   cove   t   r   age bu   t
    swel   t   er   s here whi   t   e
       ing   o   t lance t   cu   rs   ed a
s   tim   u   l   ant   f all   e   n
th ir t e   e   n s adfa de d an e   w
          king   s   o   n   p   l a s t e   r
th   r   o   n   e   s face   the
wor   nward   enter ro   r   fo nd
th re a   t   di g its   d rown n   am es   a
b   and it   f   a   w   n e   yed
  hin   ts of poi   ign o   r   e   don t
f r   e   e   i   t   i   draw   l s of t   as hop e
va nish   e   d no e as y   s a   gai t   slate

flox dowager moot potato baleen modulates dugout butane caesarean brunt trustees tetanus
opiate proximate dumpling gyroscope peony gurney sonata paisley demean ruminant
mutant phaeton daisy chain ibis lactose squaw requiem rupee natural giraffes rosary
yucca pessimist monsoon palaver croton Dies Irae cheerleader seasoning rotunda squalor
bayonet Cyclops sarong sequins endive platitude aorta Dalai Lama alfalfa ordinary

Poised sin: deliver. Oust
blooms, redbuds. Sedate
tombs. Cure bone parole. No reply,
python livid? A drought,
a shudder ceasing, so I. Was I
heard? A man-cherub bent youth
as a dagger pausing—sent
aft: noisy, low, *new*— He rebuffed truth (an
icicle: equidist-
ant prongs): "Dirty
rules operate aloof,
de-limb, yet dictate saving
morals, wield a pent sun
in iron, or swindle worth: e-
phemeral laugh,
eon love. Thaw to rinse
exiled prisons of death-
trade, a shame cunning ed-
ucated bald men
wave, favor (*their* strife:
to ply an erring thought that
oafs covet). Rage but
swelters here, white
ingot, lancet cursed: a
stimulant fallen."
Thirteen sad, faded anew
kings on plaster
thrones face the
worn warden, terror-fond
threat. Digits drown names. A
bandit fawn-eyed
hints of po— I ignore. "Don't
free it," I drawl soft as hope
vanished. "No easy saga. It's late."

            si   l ver   us
    b   om   b   s   .
            Cur b   par le   y
            v   A   r
                  i   a
                n c eru   nt
        a dag er   us   e
            s low *e*   r   tru   an
                  t
            o g   r
        es   ra   l
        li   e d   vi
        o   l   e   nt un
    i   on   s   d e   e
    p   m   al a
                              i se
              is   th
        e   sham   in   d
    uc   ed   me
                  r   *e* strif
          l   e   th ug
        s cove   Rage but
          ters   re   i
        g   n e   rse
        mula t   e
                  s   fa
    king   p a   r
        ro   t e
                  d   error f
        e   D   dro n   es A
    ba   t
        t o   I   r
    re   d   l o   op
          h   o   l e

si   l ver   us
b om   b s
    Cur b   par le   y
    v   A r
    i   a
    n c eru   nt
a dag er   us   e
    s low *e*   r   tru   an
    t
    o g   r
es   ra   l
li   e d   vi
o l   e   nt un
i   on   s d e   e
p   m al a
    i se
    is   th
e   sham   in d
uc ed   me
    r   *e* strif
l   e   th ug
s cove   Rage but
    ters   re   i
g   n e   rse
mula t   e
    s   fa
king   p a   r
ro   t e
    d   error f
e   D   dro n   es A
ba   t
    t o   I   r
re   d l o   op
    h   o   l e

odometer ulcer unicorn inlaid bronco lacerate preen lantern ichor Yale
vicuña dolor garish levitate Herod custard veldt inured yule
salamander awesome donut gonad vegetate greased sacred sleuth ulna
Siamese magic brash vicar vacant curlers banana rudder levees

Silver U.S. bombs
curb parley, variance.
Runt adage:
Ruses lower
truant ogres.
Rallied violent
unions, deep malaise,
is the sham.
Induced merest
rifle-thugs.
Coverage
butters reigners,
emulates faking,
parroted, error-
fed drones.
Abattoir: red
loop-hole.

ONI BUCHANAN is a poet and concert pianist. She holds a B.A. in English and music from the University of Virginia, an M.F.A. in poetry from the Iowa Writers' Workshop, and a Master's degree in piano performance from the New England Conservatory of Music. Her first poetry book, *What Animal,* was published in 2003. As a concert pianist, she has released three solo piano CDs and actively performs across the U.S. and abroad. She lives in Boston, maintains a private piano teaching studio, and serves as an online poetry mentor for the Anna Akhmatova Foundation.

Pursuit of a Wound
Sydney Lea (2000)

The Pebble: Old and New Poems
Mairi MacInnes (2000)

Chance Ransom
Kevin Stein (2000)

House of Poured-Out Waters
Jane Mead (2001)

The Silent Singer: New and
  Selected Poems
Len Roberts (2001)

The Salt Hour
J. P. White (2001)

Guide to the Blue Tongue
Virgil Suárez (2002)

The House of Song
David Wagoner (2002)

X =
Stephen Berg (2002)

Arts of a Cold Sun
G. E. Murray (2003)

Barter
Ira Sadoff (2003)

The Hollow Log Lounge
R. T. Smith (2003)

In the Black Window: New and
  Selected Poems
Michael Van Walleghen (2004)

A Deed to the Light
Jeanne Murray Walker (2004)

Controlling the Silver
Lorna Goodison (2005)

Good Morning and Good Night
David Wagoner (2005)

American Ghost Roses
Kevin Stein (2005)

Battles and Lullabies
Richard Michelson (2005)

Visiting Picasso
Jim Barnes (2006)

The Disappearing Trick
Len Roberts (2006)

Sleeping with the Moon
Colleen J. McElroy (2007)

Expectation Days
Sandra McPherson (2007)

Tongue & Groove
Stephen Cramer (2007)

A Map of the Night
David Wagoner (2008)

Immortal Sofa
Maura Stanton (2008)

NATIONAL POETRY SERIES

Eroding Witness
Nathaniel Mackey (1985)
Selected by Michael S. Harper

Palladium
Alice Fulton (1986)
Selected by Mark Strand

Cities in Motion
Sylvia Moss (1987)
Selected by Derek Walcott

The Hand of God and a Few
Bright Flowers
William Olsen (1988)
Selected by David Wagoner

The Great Bird of Love
Paul Zimmer (1989)
Selected by William Stafford

Stubborn
Roland Flint (1990)
Selected by Dave Smith

The Surface
Laura Mullen (1991)
Selected by C. K. Williams

The Dig
Lynn Emanuel (1992)
Selected by Gerald Stern

My Alexandria
Mark Doty (1993)
Selected by Philip Levine

The High Road to Taos
Martin Edmunds (1994)
Selected by Donald Hall

Theater of Animals
Samn Stockwell (1995)
Selected by Louise Glück

The Broken World
Marcus Cafagña (1996)
Selected by Yusef Komunyakaa

Nine Skies
A. V. Christie (1997)
Selected by Sandra McPherson

Lost Wax
Heather Ramsdell (1998)
Selected by James Tate

So Often the Pitcher Goes to Water
    until It Breaks
Rigoberto González (1999)
Selected by Ai

Renunciation
Corey Marks (2000)
Selected by Philip Levine

Manderley
Rebecca Wolff (2001)
Selected by Robert Pinsky

Theory of Devolution
David Groff (2002)
Selected by Mark Doty

Rhythm and Booze
Julie Kane (2003)
Selected by Maxine Kumin

Shiva's Drum
Stephen Cramer (2004)
Selected by Grace Schulman

The Welcome
David Friedman (2005)
Selected by Stephen Dunn

Michelangelo's Seizure
Steve Gehrke (2006)
Selected by T. R. Hummer

Veil and Burn
Laurie Clements Lambeth (2007)
Selected by Maxine Kumin

Spring
Oni Buchanan (2008)
Selected by Mark Doty

OTHER POETRY VOLUMES

Local Men and *Domains*
James Whitehead (1987)

Her Soul beneath the Bone:
    Women's Poetry on Breast Cancer
Edited by Leatrice Lifshitz (1988)

Days from a Dream Almanac
Dennis Tedlock (1990)

Working Classics: Poems on
    Industrial Life
*Edited by Peter Oresick and
    Nicholas Coles* (1990)

Hummers, Knucklers, and Slow Curves:
    Contemporary Baseball Poems
Edited by Don Johnson (1991)

The Double Reckoning of
    Christopher Columbus
Barbara Helfgott Hyett (1992)

Selected Poems
Jean Garrigue (1992)

New and Selected Poems, 1962–92
Laurence Lieberman (1993)

The Dig and *Hotel Fiesta*
Lynn Emanuel (1994)

For a Living: The Poetry of Work
Edited by Nicholas Coles and Peter Oresick (1995)

The Tracks We Leave:
Poems on Endangered Wildlife of North America
Barbara Helfgott Hyett (1996)

Peasants Wake for Fellini's *Casanova* and Other Poems
Andrea Zanzotto; edited and translated by John P. Welle and Ruth Feldman; drawings by Federico Fellini and Augusto Murer (1997)

Moon in a Mason Jar and *What My Father Believed*
Robert Wrigley (1997)

The Wild Card: Selected Poems, Early and Late
Karl Shapiro; edited by Stanley Kunitz and David Ignatow (1998)

Turtle, Swan and *Bethlehem in Broad Daylight*
Mark Doty (2000)

Illinois Voices: An Anthology of Twentieth-Century Poetry
Edited by Kevin Stein and G. E. Murray (2001)

On a Wing of the Sun
Jim Barnes (3-volume reissue, 2001)

Poems
William Carlos Williams; introduction by Virginia M. Wright-Peterson (2002)

Creole Echoes: The Francophone Poetry of Nineteenth-Century Louisiana
Translated by Norman R. Shapiro; introduction and notes by M. Lynn Weiss (2003)

Poetry from *Sojourner:*
A Feminist Anthology
Edited by Ruth Lepson with Lynne Yamaguchi; introduction by Mary Loeffelholz (2004)

Asian American Poetry:
The Next Generation
Edited by Victoria M. Chang; foreword by Marilyn Chin (2004)

Papermill: Poems, 1927–35
Joseph Kalar; edited and with an Introduction by Ted Genoways (2005)

The University of Illinois Press
is a founding member of the
Association of American University Presses.

Composed in 11/14 Adobe Garamond Pro
by Jim Proefrock at the University of Illino
Designed by Oni Buchanan and Copenhav
Mandrake photo on page iii courtesy of Ro
Part title mandrake photos © istock.com
Manufactured by Sheridan Books, Inc.

UNIVERSITY OF ILLINOIS PRESS
1325 South Oak Street   Champaign, IL 61
www.press.uillinois.edu